One Sky to the Next

PRAISE FOR
One Sky to the Next

These incredibly generous poems are challenging and comforting at once, thanks to Buckley's brilliant ability to consider, contain and invoke in a way that includes us all.
—**Naomi Shihab Nye**

Buckley is a poet, critic, essayist, and editor whose work never disappoints. He consistently writes multi-paged poems that take you on unexpected journeys that startle and delight.
—**Barbara Crooker,** interview in *Rattle*

One Sky to the Next

poems by

Christopher Buckley

Longleaf | Press
Fayetteville, North Carolina

Copyright © 2023 by Christopher Buckley

All rights reserved.

Printed in the United States of America

Cover Art: "Palatine 1, gouache" by Nadya Brown

Library of Congress Catalog Data:

Buckley, Christopher

One Sky to the Next: Poems.

ISBN: 978-1-7343985-3-3 (paperback)

Cover design by Crystal Simone Smith

Book design by Shannon C. Ward

For author inquiries or for information about permission to reproduce selections from this book contact:

Longleaf Press

Fayetteville, North Carolina

Email: longleafpress@gmail.com

Acknowledgments

Gratitude to the editors of the following journals in which these poems first appeared, often in earlier versions.

Alligator Juniper	Articles of Faith
The American Journal of Poetry	Elegies
The American Poetry Review	Devotionless
Birmingham Poetry Review	Sky Grammar;
	From Here on Out
Blue Collar Review	Climate Change
Catamaran	*Immortals' Mountain with Pavilion*
Chicago Quarterly Review	Beneath a Cemetery Overlooking the Beach
Cloudbank	Jardin du Luxembourg;
	Guardian Angel
Connecticut River Review	*Yo estoy de paso e no mas miro*
Crosswinds Poetry Journal	No Other Life
The Georgia Review	*El olor de las peluquerias me hace llorar a gritos.*
I-70 Review	Parochial Science;
	Thrift Shop Chinese Vase
Interlitq	10th Year, Drought;
	Promise
The Louisville Review	Ars Poetica
The New Guard	*Soy el mismo hasta ahorra*
New Letters	Life with Hemingway
Parhelion	*Yo paseo;*
	The World is the Last Paradise;
	To Pablo;
	Early Study;
	Evening Walk;
	Revelation
Passager	On Montecito Peak;
	Photo with Cézanne
Ploughshares	On the Air
Pedestal	All the While

San Pedro River Review	Having Said
Sky Island Journal	Perseid Meteor Shower
Solo Voyage	At Caffé Puccini
Spectrum	Likely as Not
Third Coast	Science, Clouds, & *Antoine Lavoisier*
Valparaiso Poetry Review	Prayer in Doubt

"Ars Poetica" was a *Verse Daily* selection, April 2022. Thanks to The Last Press, & QUIRE for a letterpress poetry tract of "All the While." Deep gratitude to Gary Young for decades of friendship and editing; to Mark Jarman, Gary Soto, Garrett Hongo, & Christopher Howell for friendship and encouragement; and as always to Nadya Brown for years of help & support. Special thanks to Roger Weingarten for a keen editing of the manuscript.

caminante, no hay camino, se hace camino al andar.

—Antonio Machado

CONTENTS

I
EARLY STUDY	1
ON MONTECITO PEAK	3
ON THE AIR	6
REVELATION	8
YO PASEO	10
THRIFT SHOP CHINESE VASE	12
HAVING SAID	13
THE WORLD IS THE LAST PARADISE	15

II
ELEGIES	19
SALINAS AGONISTES	23
GUARDIAN ANGEL	26
LIFE WITH HEMINGWAY	28
PHOTO WITH CÉZANNE	30
EL OLOR DE LAS PELUQUERIAS ME HACE LLORAR A GRITOS.	32
ARS POETICA	34
WINTER ON THE PATIO WITH PO CHU-I	36

III
ARTICLES OF FAITH	41
SCIENCE, CLOUDS, & *ANTOINE LAVOISIER*	43
CLIMATE CHANGE	45
PAROCHIAL SCIENCE	47
10TH YEAR, DROUGHT	49
IMMORTALS' MOUNTAIN WITH PAVILION	51
YO ESTOY DE PASO E NO MAS MIRO	53

INSUFFICIENT SKY	55
IV	
EVENING WALK	59
LIKELY AS NOT	62
FORTUNE TELLING	63
NO OTHER LIFE	65
PERSEID METEOR SHOWERS	66
PRAYER IN DOUBT	68
DEVOTIONLESS	70
SKY GRAMMAR	72
V	
SOY EL MISMO HASTA AHORA	79
AT CAFFÉ PUCCINI—NOTES ON MY 60TH BIRTHDAY	81
FROM HERE ON OUT	83
PROMISE	86
BENEATH A CEMETERY OVERLOOKING THE BEACH	88
TO PABLO	90
JARDIN DU LUXEMBOURG	91
ALL THE WHILE	93

*In memory of Jon, Omar, Peter, Phil &
Gerald Stern*

I

Early Study

I followed the currents in my texts
like a fish in the vast Bible of the sea,
made my best guesses week to week,
and loose and reckless in my bones,
took my chances between
the tides and the connective
tissue of clouds.
                    I raced around
like a halfwit with his hair on fire
until I rested beneath the coral trees
to think about where the past had gone.
But no matter how still I sat,
considering the possible outcomes
on earth, it all went speeding away
before me.
              Even so, I kept the wild
tangerines and wind-tipped bamboo
in mind, the elaboration of jacarandas,
their bruise-colored blossoms amending
the air as I rode my bike down sun-brazed lanes
long after the Assyrians had descended
on the plains and the Chaldeans destroyed
the temple at Jerusalem.
                    I'd taken notes
in Religion and General Science class
which had me chasing after the disbanded
atoms of infinity, some starlit threads . . .
after significance as invisible as salt
on sea air, as wind in white caps off shore.

Now, it looks like that's been my subject
all along, as improbable as song titles
in the '50s—*Time on my hands, I've Got
the World on a String, All or Nothing at All*—

but always a hidden meaning that
found me empty-handed, searching
for any sentiment in the subtext of light.

On Montecito Peak

> Backs on fire, our futures hard-edged and sure to arrive.
> —Charles Wright

There I was, at the edge
                of the sky . . .
                                  despite Zeno's insistence
that I'd never make it to the top—
                      the arrow across the stadium, half
of half way, ad infinitum. . . .
                      So much for theory
in its Ionian gown,
           its initial disguise.

3 hours to the peak,
                legs burning, angst of clouds rumbling
in my lungs.
        A crown of sweat on my forehead
                                    lifting
like mist off the oaks,
                until it was clear that whatever
The Meek inherit,
            it would never be this sparkling coast,
those haciendas
            fringed with lemon and jacaranda.

I knew the sophistry
            of fractions,
                      the heart counting its way
out alongside clusters of ceanothus
                      blue as quasars
billions of years
            beyond our immediate grief.
                            Overhead,
just the old company of clouds,
                the respiration of the dead

above their bodies.
                      So much for the world,
                                              I think they said.
    *

I absorbed the long view,
                      the elemental extravagance of air
where we know ourselves
                            as well as the galaxies
pulsing in their bright nets
                            like so many nerve endings . . .
where we work out the arithmetic of stars,
                                    the celestial chalk
marks of saints.
              So much for detachment.

                  *

A wretched soul in a raincoat
                        living at the trailhead
in an abandoned truck,
                huddled around his forbidden fire,
tipped a green bottle up
                like a trumpet announcing the end
of days, and disappeared
                      in the smoke as I walked by.
He'd had a clear view each night
                          to the mad bright head
of Hyakutake . . . its fizzy white light
                            like a lost wing, a smear
of silver nitrate
            cauterizing the dark—
                            thousands of years
to the other side.
            So much for time.

I doubt he's come to expect much
                      from a sky that apportioned
the poverties here below.
                I doubt the abstract comforts of philosophy
kept bitterness even marginally away,
                          shining past a parochial sea

where once we were sure
            of the results by the Aegean.

Oh, that dream
            of the shadow of smoke—
                        so much for hope . . .
starlight balancing out there
            like candles floating
                        in paper sacks
sent from the creek mouth
            out to sea.
                  So much for souls.
                  *
Hadn't I had enough?
            Not by half.
                        Though new points of pain appear—
hamstring, bone spur, arrhythmic beats.
                        You recover nothing
but your breath,
            until you don't. . . .
                        Avatars and ascended masters
sit and slow their pulses
            in such altitudes, in contemplation,
in cloud banks
            where nothing is heard of the traffic of the world,
of diminished anthems,
            the grievances of trees. . . .
For a few minutes, I rested,
            breathing pure, untarnished air,
facing in the direction
            of unqualified light—
                        its glaze igniting
palms along the shore . . .
            not that unlike the stars that continue
to find their way
            each night, all the way across the sky.

On the Air

In my perfect 6-year-old French
I sang *Frère Jacques, Frère Jacques.
Dormez-vous?* before the white caps
and the waves' salt spray—
the only song I knew
to the end, the only world. . . .

Sun burned through the mist,
white as a Eucharist,
obscure as everything I hoped
to understand . . . I was digging
a hole in the sand that the tide
never filled—wind stripping
down the eucalyptus
on the cliffs, 60 years ago. . . .

Whatever I know now
of philosophy, it seems its pages
have opened to leaves trailing
nothing more than nostalgia
all the way back along a path
bright with morning glories
and nasturtium.
                    So this morning,
stepping out onto the porch, whistling
that children's song, there seems little
to know beyond this throng of bushtits
happy with their chitter in the trees
where I can still hear fog dripping
in the camphor leaves,
the station wagon crunching
up the drive as my parents leave
for work. . . .
                    I look out above
the marine layer just offshore

absorbing every groundless theory
for our lives . . . nothing more
than a line of bird song
between then and now,
a few phrases passing on the air. . . .

Revelation

When the sun turned from the palm tree
toward the past, who knew what was coming?

All I had was a phrase in Latin about the passing
glory of the world. I bought a paper, a panatela,

a lottery ticket with the date of my birth; yet even if
the cosmos rolled my numbers out and I could afford

a '57 Impala with wings rising rapturously at the back,
it's too late for things to change. I can barely recall

cruising State, the street narrowed now for restaurants
pushing their tables out front; too late to look for

anyone I might know on the sidewalks. So I park in
the shoreline lot, sunset flashing off the pitted chrome

of my old beater like a lost passage of revelation—
so much for rebuilt dreams. I open the paper, skip

the Travel Section, Financial pages, and turn to
the horoscope—every one of us spinning away

to nowhere among the stars. . . . I scan the column
75 Years Ago Today for anything remotely familiar,

light-up, and follow the smoke rings' empty route
to the infinite, to the limits of the blue . . . dust

weighing in, the sea-heavy root of all that's gone . . .
clouds smudging the horizon like our palm prints

on the chalk board back in school. . . . And when
the stars swing down, what's your best guess about

where they're headed? Above me, on the phone line,
a mourning dove seems almost content . . . my heart,

with its own grey feathers, counting on little more
than the fellowship of air, the unattainable light.

Yo paseo

Yo paseo con calma, con ojos, con zapatos,
con furia, con olvido
                    —Neruda

Out early, I'm arm in
arm with the damp shadows
before they disappear
in the heat, while I'm still
calm, and before I forget
something else. . . .
My intention is to leave
the remorse I share with the sea
behind, though the marine layer
weighs on my shoulders, pulls
at my hamstrings whenever
I bend to admire the day lilies
just opening to the sun.

A week ago I thought
I glimpsed my father
in that tiny coffee shop
on Carrillo, tapping his college ring
on the counter along to
Andre Kostelanetz and his orchestra
over the Muzak—and every
now and then, I see my mother
window shopping on State Street,
in front of I. Magnin
for nothing she can afford.
I'm walking downtown,
toward the sea, and must
look like some city inspector
checking store fronts for cracks
and water stains, trying to

remember what used to be
there.
        But it's no use
wondering where time has gone,
or the lilacs, the loquats
crushed on the sidewalks . . .
metaphysics coming to
nothing more than an itch
at the back of my neck.
I continue in the same dust-
colored coat and shoes
as spindrift is tossed up
from rocks, the air stretching
to a point on the horizon
where I just can't see
any farther, though I do my best
to recall whatever I can
before the remaining bits
and pieces of memory
fade with the light,
with a last supplication
of acacia leaves . . .
our breath evaporating,
drifting toward the burning
spokes of stars, the furious silence
everything's headed for. . . .

Thrift Shop Chinese Vase

The birds are symbols
of prosperity, blue smudges
in a white diminished sky . . .
and the three men
beneath a tree's bare limbs
seem familiar . . .
passing cups of wine
around a small fire
where they've been sitting
for a thousand years.
With them, I look up
after the grey
strings of smoke
dissolving in the air. . . .

On the bottom,
a circle of ink around
a hut of sticks—
the potter's mark?
The tag with a red slash
tells me it's ½ price today,
due, perhaps, to the crack
like a black thread
running through
plum blossoms
on the other side.
      Still,
at $5.99 I place it in my cart—
unable to overlook the splendor,
the quiet wisdom
that shows the value
of following a vague line
of hills to the horizon,
asking myself,
what might finally
be true?

Having Said

> *Yo naci un dia*
> *que Dios estuvo enfermo*—César Vallejo

that on the day you were born
God was sick, it's easy to believe
it's only the anarchy
of imagination that keeps us
moving from the bus station
to the boardwalk, past sea wrack,
rip tide, undertow, and the oxidation
of our bones . . . waves pausing,
a little spindrift stammering
perhaps in someone else's poem?

Long ago, I collected the few bits
of luck I had coming and used them
beneath the indigent stars—the scrawls
of milky ink just castoffs of grace. . . .

Now I walk the tide line, side-stepping
tar, broken shells, like a man trying
to avoid an invisible illness on the air,
one that could certainly take him
beyond the waves . . . but no further.

I find a bench by the cliff beneath
stars that have always guided me
to a bench by the cliff, and build
a small fire of driftwood, leaves,
and can see no reason to beg
the heavens for more philosophies.

Whatever I come up with,
the wind will lay down or rise
along the shore where I stand

despite the fact that I'm up to here
among dust and the exegesis of salt,
traveler with a suitcase
of useless remedies we each
carry for ourselves, alone. . . .

The World is the Last Paradise

ay ese mundo es la victoria,
        es el paraiso perdido
                            —Neruda

I placed my faith in trees,
in the kingdom of oxygen
in parks, at the beach . . .
I was crazy
about the reservoirs
of air seeded here
and there with light,
the wings of my lungs
in full reciprocation
to the sky.
            Dreaming
the roads of my youth,
I came over the foothills
at dusk, confronting the erratic
signatures of fireflies, meteors
sprayed hugger-mugger
across the dark.
                Lavish savannahs,
the sky shifting, hoisting its sails
and moving off . . . sea foam
clinging to salt air as if
there were a purpose
to my scattered thoughts,
the unmendable darkness
stretching past the loose
pledges of galaxies. . . .

Machado told himself
that there is no road, that
you make the road by walking.
And so I don't want to sit

by the shore again looking
at the horizon and appraising
my theoretical chances.
I want to forget the inevitable
10 steps that led to the fall
of Rome along with every
Chamber of Commerce justification
for outsourcing manufacturing
of t-shirts, tennis shoes, and god-
knows-what all else to
the Mauritius Islands.
                                Each day
I do what I can to interpret
another finch song despite
the dark that carries no news
about the outcome of our blood,
an ossuary for light. One rationale
by the shore makes no more sense
than the next one—the clamor
of waves, spray, the wind
with its inevitable down-beat
and impossible wings.
                                   Unless
that's the ontological clock ticking
away in the middle of nowhere
out there . . . the rust of time
on my hands from a childhood
where we were all misled
by clouds, by every
ostensible star.

II

Elegies

> *En esta tarde, todos, todos passan*
> *sin preguntarme ni pedirme nada.*
>   —César Vallejo

Jon Veinberg 1947-2017

I close my eyes wishing
it was Spain—30 years ago—
afternoons in Menorca, with sherry,
plates of tapas, with my wife
and my best friend,
still some blanks on my life-
list of complaints . . .
nothing needed
for happiness beyond
those last scraps of youth—
but who knew that then,
with no jack-knifed backbones,
no irreparable ligaments
of despair?
    Living check to
check, drinking cheap wine,
I was at least not exiled
to the park all day, alone
like our impoverished maestro,
Vallejo—compatriot of the twig,
amicus to the court of crumbs,
thread-bare before the wind—
Vallejo with nowhere to go,
and no means to get there,
worrying an end of bread
and leaf-thin slice of cheese
through the afternoon. . . .

I was alive in the lavish
Iberian light and possessed
enough *pesetas* to sing out
*tortilla patata, jamon serano,
camarones a la plancha* . . .
drawing on an old account
with the clouds as they stood in
for all that had gone missing
since I was 6—everything I'd filed
in the index of the blue
despite the immediate images
of whitecaps slipping beneath
the swells.   I salute each cloud
drifting across the dusk,
dingy as an old sheet
but calling to mind
each *compadre*, each ghost
sailing by autumn's windowsill,
past the possibility of a soul—
old handkerchief stuffed
in the inner pocket
of my coat. . . .   Who can say
if they still know us, love us,
how that might stand up
against the Tramontana wind
as it hollows out the waves?
Now, if not for this bench
above the sea, where
would I turn for solace
from the falling leaves,
how would I manage the sinking
feeling in my blood at the end
of each day?   I meant to
have something figured out

before sitting down
to recall a few passages
from dry eucalyptus limbs
rubbing along in wind,
speaking song-like in what
sounds like *Catalan*?

I shrug my shoulders, knowing
I have no wings, but feeling
exactly what Vallejo meant
when he said, *I have put
my upper arm bones on wrong* . . .
the clouds drifting
beyond my reach, the sky
not much shifted beyond
the '30s where I missed
my chance to share a little wine
at a café table in Paris
with him, discussing the saints
who had left us
walking the cemeteries and
wet streets alone.
                      The stars
haven't moved any more than
the sediment in our bones,
dust consigned like wishes,
like pinwheels barely sparkling
into the night where anyone
who looks closely can see
the details were never
there.
        Theoretical physicists,
philosophers, exalted exegetes
of nucleic acid, why
is the equation of transience so
unsolvable?
                Best guess,

there could be a boneyard
of light where we'll meet up,
broken or whole, in bits
and pieces, in packets or waves,
with any particles or crusts
of prayer left to the sky.

For now, I have to remind myself
that I am not sick, nor more
heart-sore than anyone else
occupying a municipal bench—
that I have to do what I can
to admire the eucalyptus,
their high white crowns
singing back the sea clouds'
indecipherable
context of our hope.

Salinas Agonistes

Blind among enemies, O worse than chains, / dungeon, or beggery, or decrepit age! —Milton

Luis Omar Salinas 1937-2008

Our guardian angels
         all took the Greyhound to Mazatlan,
except that *viejo*
         asleep in his pick-up
                behind the Rexall drug—
Jorge Negrete on the radio
         with *No Te Rajes*
                circulating forever
in my Aztec blood.
         I stumbled along
                in my impoverished shoes,
singing to every Mary and Martha,
                to the sorrowful mysteries
of their necks.
         Midnight romantic,
                I climbed the bougainvillea
to balconies,
         a pack of KOOLS,
                beer in a sack, the corporal works
of mercy as I knew them. . . .
                I drove with one hand over an eye
of my double-vision youth,
         tipped my hat
                and ashes of moonlight
tumbled out.
         I valorized the blossoms of the apricot,
                my soul
on all fours, floating
         like a sandwich wrapper in wind
over to Roeding Park
         where I spent my days matriculating

with the larks,
         learning all I could about hope.
                       All through the '80s
I couldn't tell
      one neorealistic misery from the next—
                         Visconti's from
De Sica's—the emotional sprockets and chain links,
                        but knew
they cut an hour from Bertolucci's U.S. release of *1900*,
and years before,
           I'd hit the road, making soup with Tony Quinn
in black & white
       along the Adriatic coast.
                       I returned to the sea—
my reservoir of dreams—unfurled a white sail
                     before the existential waves
and my heart capsized in moonlight
               despite having nothing left to lose.

Adios amigos—
      no melodies are left
           in the waves,
                 and the stars
always did their best
      to keep me off course.
                 If it takes a fool
to be a poet, I deceived no one,
         as I went in search of roses
not philosophy,
      which I had freely
           each day from sparrows in the yard.

I left the sport coat of fame
          in the display window, no inheritance
but the *gritos* of the gulls.
           Somewhere, there are silver trumpets
and mariachis singing
      El Rancho Grande, but I can't hear them

from here.
        I bequeath my manuscripts to the thrift shop
of the wind
            and am going to hitch-hike to the stars.
                            My parents
took the package tour to paradise
                        and put a word in for me,
but God, it seems, is not sentimental.
                        You wouldn't think so,
but I loved him well enough
            in my own way—
                        no other choice
left for a *desgraciado*
            still standing in the street?

Guardian Angel

Sister Caritas insisted we each had one, right
behind us with a scorecard, with help resisting
temptation—what little was available back then.
Mine ducked out early—climbed a boxcar
to look for work in the strawberry fields near
Guadalupe, or as night clerk in a rooming house
in Saticoy while I cruised State Street in a '56 Bel Air
with my *compadres*, trying to get through things
as fast as we could. . . .
                                  Decades down the road
I'd forgotten all the orthodox claptrap until one day
my heart did double-takes—the mechanic with
my retreating hairline, my beard, with a little wound
of ink or motor oil leaking from his breast pocket,
worrying me—a silver pool of anti-freeze at his feet,
which, in one world or another, indicates an accident,
a fall from grace. He passed a rag the color of old fire
over a break drum until it took on a beatific gleam,
tapped embers from his pipe before turning back
to his machines and rust, humming "My Blue Heaven,"
content with the broken struts and tail pipes of the road—
a life, given my miserable performances in science and math,
that could easily have been mine had I stayed put.
And though we're equally light in the wallet,
one of us knows the scale and dynamics of wind
and the other his cheerless part in gravity.
                                             Last time
in town I found myself brooding on side streets,
staring through silted windows at Old Doc's Liquors,
the Chicken Pie Shop for a face I might know. Yes,
of course—he never left Fresno, its flat linen light
and freight yards, its seraphic miles of almonds and plums,
crepe myrtle, and fig, Basque restaurant with 7-course
sheep-herder meals for little more than a prayer.

He never stood in line for career advancement, a step
up the ladder of merit, a step back, the greasy pole . . .
never moved from the bottom of Arthur Street, not far
from the Eagle Café or the music store with the piano
for sale in its picture window for a dozen years.
He's still a stone's throw from the tracks, just across
from the pitiful zoo where peacocks, calling over
the redwoods like abandoned souls, don't bother him
a bit. He bends a knee, confides to the last irises,
their white and topaz wings; he tends his runner beans,
his chilies . . . slices one, tests it on his tongue
in hope of speaking with the birds, asking them
to pardon the fruiting mulberry, the three
slender nectarines on the left.
                                   His Nikes slouch
on the porch, old gold ones with waffle tread,
slim blue wings along the sides . . . ones he slips on
for a run, flying up past Palm then back down
to Olive, to Piemonte's where he still gets away with
mortadella and provolone, bottles of thick Italian red—
he's not worrying himself to death about his health.
Home, he tears a few yellow pages out of an old
Latin text to start a yard fire in the back for
the brown tomato leaves and grocery sack of weeds,
pushes up his sleeves, disappearing with his paper-white
skin into the smoke, only to reappear at the picnic table
with a water glass of that red wine—minor miracle
of the suburbs. . . .
                            He hums along with Pavarotti
on his cassette player, happy for a Saturday, the grey
peace of early fall, glad for this slab of land picked up
before everyone invested in real estate and IPOs.
I look closer, comparing our bear-like slump,
the short wingspan of our arms as he stands back up
too quickly and a lightness rushes through my bones
as I feel the sweep of clouds ascending in my head. . . .

Life with Hemingway

I'm at my local *taqueria* for *salsa* acetylene,
Trio Los Panchos on the jukebox from the '50s
when I look up from a plate of *chorizo con heuvos*
to my reflection in the window, and there, in khaki cap
and a safari shirt with cargo pockets and epaulets,
(picked up cheap at a Charity shop), is someone
with a grizzled beard looking a hell of a lot more
like Hemingway than Hugh Grant with his
frothy mane of hair.
      And before either Hugh
or I know it, I'll have passed Hemingway's last
miserable year when he couldn't think, write,
or piss straight, when I'm telling myself that 2
out of 3's not bad.
      Each year now when I open
In Our Time to that fourth short interchapter
with "young Buckley" coming in with his patrol,
and German soldiers "potted" as they came over
the wall, I tell the students I barely knew him then,
stood to the back in the regimental photo—you can
hardly tell it's me . . . and they miss the gag completely,
look out the windows the way they gaze at clouds
over the Apennines on their summer holidays—
dismissing the possibility of war ever coming for them.

But wouldn't I'd go back in a minute to cruise
the Caribbean, to scout U-boats on *Pilar*, or to light
the hurricane lamps around *Finca Vigia* each evening,
a double corona from *Vuelta Abajo*. And why ever
leave Havana—old Soldiers of the Republic in the streets
spitting any time names of Fascists are heard—there's
that Miro on the wall, the celestial rum, the mails
working more or less. If I sent Fidel a villanelle
denouncing Late Capitalism, maybe he'd invite me

for daiquiris overlooking *Playa Paraiso* where there's
not one bonfire along the sand, nothing but a barefoot kid
with a flashlight looking for a baseball in the undergrowth,
the starry sky south of town. . . .
                                      I'm not going
to Sweden to accept a prize, not heading to Harvard for
my honorary degree, and why get on a plane again
to Miami to read to 20 people in a classroom? No reason
to leave California for NYC and go a few more rounds
with the boys in bow ties to see if the acid still rises
in the blood like a toreador's.
                                  No one sidesteps
the horns of time, that hooking motion waiting
to blind-side you from the shadows of afternoon.
Better to sit in the stands, in the shade, in a backwater
like Lompoc, where they wouldn't know Hemingway
from Howard Hughes. Better to light up a Montecristo,
the one I'm not allowed this month, and settle for
no one, not even God, looking over my shoulder.

Photo with Cézanne

Yes, that's me, standing
next to Paul Cézanne
in 1 of his 20-some self-portraits.
And though not quite as bald,
there's a camaraderie
in the humility of our scalps,
in the crosshatched brush strokes
of middle age . . . a few sticks
of landscape in the background
for atmosphere—beige and grey
as Lompoc, more than several
bucolic degrees of separation
from his home at *Jas de Bouffan*.

But the dark impassive eyes . . .
there's something we have
in common, even as I looked beyond
the clouds shifting above my reflection
in Woolworth's window, age 5 . . .
in the mirror this morning,
combing what hair there's left—
easy to see myself fading
into the violet shade
of poplars, into the sky's watery
skein, that vague relief cast against
our desire, returning each evening
like a crow into the pines—twilight
polished with mist, nostalgias
drifting in . . . we're only so
many minerals ground
usefully with oil—minor
significances of water
and salt, temporary traces of light,
glossed, and as much at risk as

the trees with their last dark thoughts,
as the river carrying off everything
to the empty horizon . . . which
he chose to make it clear
that one day you reach a point
where there's little left
to hide behind any more.

> *El olor de las peluquerias me hace llorar a gritos.*
> —Neruda

The smell of barbershops has me breaking out
in sobs . . . but who needs one now? Not me,
and not you in that photograph from '48—
the year I was born, a year you were pretty much
already bald. But they call back a vanished world
of Violet Water, *Tres Flores,* and Bay Rum—
a blameless childhood savoring the glassy syllables
of the sea. What dreams were left on the lips
of the wind as you looked out over water, clouds
skimming the Pacific for the next 55 years since
this grainy snap, since the last time you considered
a haircut?
          I want to reclaim that world of Vitalis
and Aqua Velva—clippers humming over our ears,
thinning shears clicking behind our heads, below
the Barbicide in tall sea-tinged jars, talc descending
like cloud dust, and that blossom of alcohol—
mist of bloated roses and musty newspapers,
chrome ashtrays standing to attention, filled with
stubs of White Owls, El Productos, and Dutch Masters.
LIFE, or the *Saturday Evening Post* in laps
of old-timers dozing in Naugahyde chairs
next to the john . . . sleepy blades of a ceiling fan
churning flies and the lives we left behind
in Temuco and Montecito.
          You escaped
to Europe on horseback over the Andes. I rode in
on the coattails of post-war economic recovery,
there, in my parents' baby pictures—I'm propped up
and happy on the hood of their new Pontiac parked
above Humboldt Bay, CA, wearing the same cap
you'd wear the next 25 years, and like you, knowing
the sound of the sea before I knew my name . . .
20 years to come before I'd know yours. And so

we're preserved for posterity, the proletariat, the glossy,
on-going album of dust—you, looking young
in middle age, younger than I've ever seen you,
younger than I am now—
         sand-colored snap, short
steel-wool beard, worker's shirt and insubordinate
glare of a defender of the oil-drowned seas, the clear-
cut trees, the rights of miners, of nitrate shovelers
in Tarapaca to sip at the honeycomb of oxygen—
for which they ran you out of the dining rooms
of *caballeros*, out of the Senate, and for which
they ate their words when yours made them infamous.
A few decades—out and back—*saludos*, and
adios.
  We dreamt on opposite sides of the sky,
where there are few barbershops these days, and
no seats in the cinema on Saturdays, no double
features and world news in black & white,
let alone wind-combed beaches reflecting the clear
thinking of the sea.
       No one knew you
looked like this—hard, rough, defiant as a root,
spinning in place with the fury of a water spout.
I knew only the image of an avuncular poet
from the back of your books, clean shaven, bald
as a pope, *brujo* with rip tides and the raging syntax
of the ocean up his sleeves.
        Who were we,
there on the edge of the sea, the sky reflecting
our untroubled visions in tide pools, in the resinous
stanzas of pines, the fair-weather clouds floating
with our hearts as we headed off to school each day,
stepping from stone to stone on our path back
to the sky, where, deep in the anonymity of air,
we looked briefly like whoever it was we then
said we were, Neftali Reyes Basoalto!

Ars Poetica
Lu Ji (261-303)

General, minister, poet, you
never had a chance . . .
A brush at the tip of your mind
touched the eight borders
of the world, all the seas—
you recognized that
there are many styles, but that
the mind requires precision.

The *Wen Fu*—your treatise on
the art of writing—was
too dazzling for a jealous
court—you were undone
by political intrigue
midway in life,
your last night on earth spent
wondering if you'd ever
again hear the cranes
of your home
in *Huading*? There
is an ode for each
cloud, all the heavens to fill
with the unflagging
attention of the heart.

A wise man
would give his life
to this instead
of the skills of war,
if he could just let
ambition drift away.

Every night
the shifting stars

remind me
we're alone
on the earth,
no matter
what we say.

Winter on the Patio with Po Chu-I

To James Wright

80° in southern California
                       and no change in sight. . . .
I've gotten nowhere
            trying to write
                      about an old governor
working his way up river, all his life. . . .
                           I should jump off
Po's raft leading back 12 hundred years
                           to a loneliness
from which no one is saved.
                   I had to watch my step
to even make it to this back-water
                      where I walk along
as waves crash into the seawall,
               dodging the spray
to find a bench where I can follow leaves
                        lifting away
in a gust with faces from the past.
                      I put in regular hours
and ask myself why everything turns up too late?
                             Finally cash
in my pocket, I buy sparkling water
                         instead of champagne,
leaving the stars to bubble and rise on their own.
                             Weather refuses
to arrive above the rose beds;
                 on the evening news, snow
continues to fall in Minneapolis.
                45 years . . . and I'm still
coming back to your poem—what's the use?
                         At the end

of the garden, liquidambars are a black scrawl
                                                        against twilight.
I look up
        and guess I'll get somewhere
                                        by dark.

III

Articles of Faith

I believe in dust,
the particle almighty,
every destructible bit
of heaven and earth . . .
in the long-shot-
fat-chance chaos
that burned down to us
with bacteria and
mitochondrial DNA,
their invisible scrawls
slipping off the clipboard
of the void. . . .
                       And
in the beginning and flat-out
flash to the end, first
and last emblems
of the emptiness where
they streaked from nothing
and flew by
the floorboards of time
down the invisible
sluiceways of dark
energy, which now
looks like most all of it—
whatever "it" might be?

I believe neutrinos
know us as angels might,
for our wobbly assemblies
of atoms—they pass
through us as easily as God
particles—confirmed
but yet unseen. . . .
It's a good blind bet—

quarks, charmed or strange,
the negative charge
of muons, the impact
carried by gauge bosons,
the scaffoldings from which
we're erected, and thus
the cathedral of the atom,
every untied force
in the unified field
cast out and falling
apart like gravity,
nevertheless holds
us here in the brief
embrace of our cells,
in eleven dimensions
undiscovered save for
some caliginous equations,
and in un-seeable strings
and parallel membranes
to be resurrected
in one star-blast or another,
and stars at best
5% of the light
almost everlasting
in its packets and waves,
in the un-sourced source,
the unknown
and approximate shores
far from anywhere
we live.

Science, Clouds, & *Antoine Lavoisier*

What, if anything, remains of us?
                                       1667 and scientists said *Phlogiston* was
the substance of fire—
               (fire that nuns said most of us lazy bodies and souls
were headed for)—
         and that it was released when objects burned—
ash equaling the essential matter . . . so there was that. . . .

Sometime earlier, Empedocles
                        maintained that burning was a process
of decomposition . . . closer to the mark?
                                Either way, no one identified
a preamble of light
           inside us, a source we eventually give up
                                         as if
we'd agreed to death?
                  We'd seen Dutch painting, peasants working
happily away in fields
             regardless of ice or fire, while the well-off
in white collars
       and death-black suits, observed
                        from a hill over the hayricks,
from the safety of a bridge
         above the dead stars
                       frozen in a river
they'd skated across for years. . . .
               Everyone was tossed a metaphysical bone—
an afterlife's shimmering concourse in the aether
                         looking just like
another assembly of clouds
            building and dissolving the way the 19th c. did,
shuffling across the low countries
           or English midlands in galvanized striations,
scumbled, rubbing along, mercury-edged.

                      Then Constable arrived

with a spiraled, cathedral shine,
                               clouds milky and glazed,
                                                               that kept you
pinned beneath their wing-spread
                              and immaculate regalia of grief,
bruise-blue at evening's edge.
                        But for once—despite Constable's clouds
out the window and my mind half a cloud then—
                                         I'd done my homework
for General Science,
               raised my hand, and in my best French accent
proclaimed,
       Antoine Lavoisier—who named oxygen and hydrogen,
gave us the molecular equation for clouds,
                         and delivered the final blow
to Phlogiston,
         proving matter changes form, and is never destroyed . . .
which, in the eyes of the nun,
                       inched me slightly back from
Purgatory's oven doors,
                 reassured me for a while that we were
what we were,
          no matter how hot things got.

Climate Change

Not a chance, they said,
      that the planet's turning,
or everything would be flung
        into space, clouds
would be ripped from the sky
        as the earth spun past.
And though Copernicus proved
        the sun was at the center
and planets rotated
     around it,
       the authorized thought—
like a body at rest—
      resisted change.
          A lot of it still about.

Push market projections along,
       but less than 5%
of the universe is matter,
       atoms reconditioned
to make us up
     so we might invest in hedge funds,
file quarterly reports,
      make hostile takeovers.
But in informed quarters
      5 will get you 10 that
it's all the result
     of a dazzling cosmic crapshoot,
a cloud now little more
       than a cup of quantum ashes
bunched across inconstant skies
        despite the ad hoc
focus group's conclusions.

      So if,
        as every CEO believes

on Sunday,
    God set every particle pin-balling about,
ordered
   the IPOs with derivatives promised
in a metaphysical futures market,
       how improvident is it
not to prize the earth above
     all else?

The dead stars continue
       to reach us with their blank checks
of light, substantial
    as every rationalization
for a gross national product,
      outsourcing, and the foreign
trade wars corporate think-tanks
     cook-up.

And despite the primary exports
      of China, Chile, Ecuador,
or Brazil, press releases say
     it all revolves around us
as oceans spin in place
     beneath a drift-net of debris—
polystyrene, plastic bottles,
    nylon rope,
       oil-brown foam
in the tide, grey moonlight—
     even if we did
walk out of the sea
    one day on our own industrious fins
with all the applied forces of desire.

Parochial Science

Einstein didn't pull up his socks
and attend temple, worry about his soul.
Instead, he played violin in the kitchen
as he worked out the math in his head—
trying to put gravity, electro-magnetism,
the weak and strong nuclear forces
back together again.
                        Once, a rabbi,
fishing for celebrity support, telegraphed
asking if he believed in God?
"I believe in Spinoza's God"—
Einstein replied—"who reveals
himself in the orderly harmony
of what exists, not in a God who
concerns himself with the fates
and actions of human beings."

The nuns couldn't explain what
held our molecules together
other than some great invisible force,
the standard myths, and yet were
sure that most of us, sitting in
even rows, in our uniform shirts,
would end up roasting on a fiery spit
for all eternity—certain they knew
what that was as well. . . .

But even before we opened our
General Science books, I had my doubts . . .
water into wine, rising from the dead—
it looked like a spiritual shakedown,
a glorified Madison Ave. campaign
for Faith and full ecclesiastical employment,
as none of them could begin to

diagram the syntax of stars—the implied
subject, the indirect and un-lasting
objects in the cosmos—any more
than they could fly to the moon.

10th Year, Drought

I put on my straw hat to hold in hope,
                                        whatever I have left
of it as I walk out past the dehydrated trees
                                              where I can't help
but think of Goya's *El tres de mayo*,
                                how, with their arms
surrendered to a black sky,
                              those anarchists look just like the trees,
slumped desperately into each other,
                                    waiting to die. . . .
Along the cliff, there's a bougainvillea,
                              blood-red through
the prickly pear,
                    humming birds at the bruise-colored blossoms
of Mexican sage—
                          and that's all it takes to have me praising what's left
before the heat arrives
                        and I toss another worthless prayer
past the islands, the crags of Santa Cruz,
                                the far reaches of San Miguel,
looking for any cloud-trace
                        slipping in from 40 years ago. . . .
But daydreaming is so much dust
                        in the rain barrel
at the corner of the house
                        where I watched B westerns,
filmed just 90 miles south,
                            which we tuned-in Saturday mornings
in black & white
                  while it rained, while clouds
                                      of dust were rising
from the posse in pursuit. . . .
                    What chance now
                                the sky's

               going to open up
                              and return us to those days?
                                                        Above the bay
               each evening, starlight blurring,
                                       burning down. . . .

Immortals' Mountain with Pavilion

California is long,
like Wen Jia's
hanging scroll....
50 years
I've driven
up and down
the coast,
windblown
as mist ... grey
ink on old paper.

Who would
be Han-Shan
or his friend
Shih-Te now,
wearing rags
in the wild,
scraping images
into bark,
into rock,
then running off,
laughing,
renouncing
all the world
in front of you?
Not many years
ago it seems,
we'd have said,
Yes, I would....

Not even
Po Chu-i
could give up
the eroding earth,

leave longing
to the rain,
as he made
that journey
up river toward
a flag of light
high in the window
of the cliff,
in the province
of lost men. . . .
Cups of wine,
evening leading
to a place where
almost all ambition
disappears.

Wind worries
the cliffs, fits
the ancient redwoods—
pale pinnacles,
a narrow trail
toward the sky—
yet still a ways
to go . . . a small
pavilion overlooking
the path . . . voices
above the skeletal
pines. And a hut
of sticks hidden
among rocks, threads
of smoke high
in the corner
of the horizon—two
figures climbing a ladder
of clouds. . . .

                for Gary Young

Yo estoy de paso e no mas miro
                            —*Jaime Sabines*

I'm walking on the breakwater, orchestrating
a low sky for rain that never falls over
acacias, over my brain going grey as those leaves.

Like Sabines, I'm passing through and just look. Down
the street, memory in a threadbare suit from
the Thrift, begins to blur . . . who knows what's lost

and what's still wavering above the palms? Should I
declare allegiance to Hopelessness, like a man
who knows no better than to reach for the roots

of the sea, for salt spray clinging briefly to
to starlit reefs? Metaphors aside,
I can feel the rust in my shoulder bones

as they give way to physics, to our immutable
quarks. But how can I disavow the bits
and pieces that have brought me this far? I can't

remember the last time someone stopped, looked
around in the park, turned and asked me,
Is this how things were supposed to turn out?

How to know if the wind is done with us? What
did we do but clamber through the time,
the sea mist of our lives—our assembled particles

and associated specks encoded to unhinge and spin
away in the sea spume and starry ellipses
of the dark? Once, the planet was covered by

the pitch and scrawl of rain, the inexhaustible
downpour of days—which, if they were
endless, no longer look that way from here. . . .

Insufficient Sky

Eucalyptus, acacia, oak—
leaves driven through the streets,
like a flurry of dead souls. . . .

In the end, we'll drift
with our lost breath, assorted
quantum bits without
a single hosanna
from the cosmos . . .
and where would that
get us anyway?

For now, azure
strata swirl and sift down
from nowhere, invisibly
covering my hands,
my shoes, as I stand
before the indifferent
sea, where I've taken
most all my risks. . . .

The guesswork lies
in what we assume
is the eternal air . . .
in what might be
eternal above the air?

In my 20s, I was sustained
by the traffic of electrons
clicking like castanets
in my blood —fearless
then as I rode the rush
of Portuguese rosé through
sunlight and corpuscular space

and felt it singing for a time
all about me. . . .
                      But now
my invocations come to
little alongside the crows
with their instinctive fury
and desire to run us off
and keep even the scrubland
secular and safe despite
our collective knowledge
that no kingdom of pity
is coming, no
compensation for
the profanity of dust,
equal to, and worthless
as our bones.
                  So how
far to the stars?
How many miles left
in these old shoes?
The longer I stand
on the breakwater
looking out at dusk
the more it seems clear
that the sky's the limit. . . .

IV

Evening Walk

Heading off into the neighborhood
I let silence take me by the elbow,
as if I'd run out of things to think,
as if my brain had been battered
by the firmament one final time. . . .
All afternoon I bothered birds
with my useless salutations—
and now it's the cocktail hour
and I can't trust myself
alone in the house, spirits
winking from the cupboard,
inviting me to forget things
for a while.   But if I get out
and get going I'll be back
to the porch with just enough time
for a glass lifted to salute the weary
shadow of the sea as it climbs
the cliff with the dark, confirming,
once again, that circumstances
are unlikely to change.
                        I stop
every 50 feet to admire the sea light
bequeathed to us by the old gods,
or the quantum field—either way,
I move along in the unsolved algebra
of my blood—who needs more
information about grief's irreducible
factors?
        The withered tamarisks
stand for all the conclusions I came to,
and crows go on listing their final
grievances from the phone pole,

from the black cypress etching
an icy moon. At 83, my mother
in her hospice bed, told me she wanted
to die—what great faith, or great lack thereof,
was that—and what possibly was left
to submit to the sky? How many hosannahs
reach the constellations before we're
forgotten for good, for any difference
it might make? So, orphans, refugees,
old-timers on the bus, have we come this far
for nothing? Does it matter that I can't recall
who taught me to tie my shoes, or when
I was apprenticed to the tide? I keep asking
myself if the sky is holding something back
for the grand immensity, or if it's just
some low clouds bruised and vanishing
at the same time each day? The trees
argue it both ways with the keepsakes
of dust. Early on, I thought I had a chance
to make some sense of things, and though
the north star hasn't wavered for centuries,
all my instruction comes to nothing
as I side-step the sanctimonious in favor of
a few hard facts—this man, for example,
in the park, stuffing newspapers from the trash
inside his coat for warmth. A falling star
shoots overhead as I make the turn for home
expecting no more joy than being someone
walking through the last hours of the day
can provide. The light sleeping in our bones
breaks down over time . . . time which
greys the edges of our photographs.
And insofar as hope is concerned—

the window-dressing of the sky—
well, it's nothing more than an oath
I swear each evening to the sea
without a witness.

Likely as not

the wind's still outside the Arlington Theater, filling
my jacket with dust after the Saturday matinee—
I could never remember where I left it? I like to think

coyotes are the last romantics, howling *Tu, Solo Tu*
whether there's a moon or not. Stars gather and subtract
all night above the foothills, where it looks like I've lost

my way forever, despite those stars strung across the night
like concertina wire, and moving away—leading us
nowhere. . . . Some believe that whatever happens is

the result of something you did before, coming back
at you, but it's only hazard, cellular degeneration,
not reincarnation. So, where have all the clouds gone?

They're supposed to keep circling, changing into our
breath, working in loose formation through our blood
from millions of years back, where scientists believe

a trace of mitochondrial DNA hopped off a comet
and got in the swim with interloping bacteria, eventually
accounting for us coming up from under the waves

on our industrious fins, for me ambling down the hallway
in the middle of the night, walking, I think, downtown by
the old storefronts—Montgomery Wards turned into a bank,

Woolworth's into a bookstore despite the gilt-edged glass
in the house-high store-front windows that captured
my reflection, age 5, along with my mother. Those

windows doing the same today, a thousand streaks
of light, my grey image imprinted against clouds—all
there is when it comes to the sum total of infinity.

Fortune Telling

> *Those who have become*
> *birds seem happy to be no longer us.*
> —Jim Harrison

No reason to complain any more
than I used to, to analyze the last
creases of light falling across the path. . . .
Once I had stars pasted on my collar

for Art and French, never thinking
I'd be one who believed there was no joy
to be found anywhere but on earth—
but who knew what was coming?

Since then, I've doubled down that
it's only mist up there and not angels
who've forgotten their assignments here.
My thoughts lift past the mares' tails

and stratus clouds heading for Canada,
look for room to breathe, for an afterlife
of air below the stars. But if I leave stars out
of the deliberations, what have I been looking at

all this time? Our bones come from the minerals
in stars, and soon we'll have to give them back.
How much light can the sky let go? Finally,
I'm making sense of the mockingbird's desperate

oratorio to life from the top of the star pine,
the camaraderie of spice finches each dusk
as they hang on to pampas plumes for dear life . . .
me too. My imminent future is breathing

alongside acacia and coral trees, congregating
happily with grackles and crows—the company,
though rowdy and ruffled, is reliable—all of us
equally bemused, staring into space, beyond

the blue and empty curve of earth with little
chance the last seabirds are bringing in news
of an afterlife as we make our best guesses,
reading more into the dark sky each day.

No Other Life

Douglas Family Preserve, Santa Barbara

Once in a while,
in autumn,
the architecture
of light climbs
the salt lattices
of mist above the sea,
the humming thread
and fabric of the blue
go still, and a throng
of cedar wax wings
appears and pours through
the wild pyracanthas
near the cliff,
stripping, from between
the leaves and thorns,
the fire-red berries that
the universe has provided
for them. . . .
                Then
they're off—certain,
it seems, of a destination,
the next assignment
for their lives . . . a little dust
blowing up from beneath
the cypresses.
                I like to
stand here and follow
the air for a while
as they lift away,
for no other reason
than this is
what I've been given
to hold on to.

Perseid Meteor Showers

The night finds us out
in the yard waiting for streaks,
the slant and shreds of ice and dust,
of light driving through us
just for show . . . scars stamped across
our occipital lobes, our eyes now
much like the thin skin over
daffodils before they burst out
in bloom. . . .
                Stars are
as scattered as the years, lost
like the sound of a sled
pulled through fresh snow,
as indecipherable . . . the world's
meaning or need long hidden
and ignored, like the hunting party
on the walls of Alta Mira,
the polychrome bison and beasts
we can no longer name. . . .

Let's suppose some radar in our brains
calls us out each time, tags the white
flashes falling against August
with an old meaning that pulses
in our wrists and has us gazing
north as if we were tied to some nebula
stumbling along but not yet
drawn into the gullet of time . . .
the murmuring of the spheres,
a music beneath which we were
once at peace sitting with a glass
of something cool, the clouds
of the past wandering through
the soul, starlight echoing

at the end of the road, heaven
rooted in nothing beyond
the reflections of our fears,
undisguised.

Prayer in Doubt

Rain on the hoods
of parked sedans
reciting novenas,
the storm trundling
down the coast
dour as the old ones
in overcoats out
from midday mass—
veils and canes,
the end of afternoon
leading nowhere
beyond simmering pots,
kitchen windows dim
as clouds.
               Let me
take the next bright thing
in the sky as a sign
our lives spiral back
to us reusable as air,
as the flung galaxies
knotted together by
some dark, invisible matter,
by any of us turning
the wind's thin page
to a hymn of light,
marking our places
beyond the last
thumb print of winter,
the smudged blue scarf
of the horizon blown
high and snagged
in the sycamores, where,
for a minute, starlings
are grinding out something

close to joy before reaffirming
that there's no easy grace
on earth, and shattering the sky
with their frantic
and faithless wings. . . .

Devotionless

En muriendo y cantando. Y bautizar la sombra . . .
—César Vallejo

Late night, even longing washed from the sky—
    it's all finally black and white . . .
        and even if the dark

is not unbounded, I go on connecting the dots
    tossed out above the shimmering
        stanzas of the sea. . . .

Wind in the mimosa with the easy habit of belief.
    There's nothing to be made of that,
        or a dead moon

at its usual remove, grey midnight clouds like
    so many hand prints high on a wall
        beyond the consequences

of light. If I overlooked the apparatus of hope—
    and so hopelessness—wouldn't I be
        just another interpreter

of wind, faithful along a weedy childhood lane,
    someone looking after shadows as they
        descend the staircase

of the sky in comfort, one of many who retrace
    the clouds, their own dim steps, off
        into the mute districts of air?

If nothing changes the past, there's nothing left to say
    in God's defense. As for history, there's not
        much left on the bones

poking through the sand. Pulp of light in my veins,
    I find myself recapitulated in the
        everlastingness of dust,

singing and dying with the sea's last offer . . . so
    what is there for me to do beneath an
        unsolved sky but take it?

Sky Grammar

Apostrophes, ellipses, ampersands . . .
           sea clouds
inscribe the fading blue . . .
       the mind making order,
             parsing
fragments, irregular forms,
       against the invisible
            backdrop of air.
A line of cumulus
      like muddled parts of speech—like knots
in a rope pulled
     and I only have the hands
           the universe gave me,
the declensions of wind
       slipping through my fingers, little remaining
outside a swirl
     of prepositions:
         on, above, before, beneath, beyond—
with, as Sister Julie said in 5th grade,
          anything you can do
to a cloud. . . .

         *

Pat your pockets . . .
      the key to the past,
         like the voyages
that becalmed you here, lost.
       What is it
         a shooting star tells you?
No help whistling *Moonlight Cocktails*,
        Serenade in Blue,
I Cover the Waterfront. . . .
      No one hears a thing
from that far back—
      the modifiers of each breath,
           the dim
and distant reverberations.

*

Over the West Side
                        cumulus like flagstones . . . ellipses
stepping off longing
                beyond the hills . . . beneath them,
the crossing
          where empty boxcars rolled through,
                                    where everything
closed at 5:00—silo, grain elevators, loading docks . . .
                                          ledgers shut,
office shades pulled down—
                    foreman, secretary, hired hands,
home for supper.
                Across the road, the woods,
                                and past that the park,
stanzas of sun-burnt grass, the spondees of peacocks
                                      complaining
in the heat. . . . Above the Tower District,
                          the same vague clouds
like clauses, like lines of cursive
                        no one cares about anymore . . .
an absence drifting by . . .
              nothing left
                        to parse on the air. . . .

Who can recall the names, the proper nouns
                                left on the side streets—
Piemonte's Deli, *carniceria*, Chicken Pie Shop,
                                the irregular variations
and night-inflected phrases
                    down the long bar in the Basque Hotel
beside glasses of *Fundador*?
                      And though there is only one conjugation
for the past, I'm working to identify
                      the voice, mood, and number
of each face vanished behind the windows,
                            the illegible clouds
                                          of silt.
I'm listening for the last suffix of desire
                        in the leaves of sycamores

and Chinese elm
                drifting down with our expectations,
                                                        40 years ago
in the park,
        the peacocks pleading each morning
                                        for mercy,
for an interjection of rain, of shade.
                              Mercy on us all. . . .

                    *

Nothing corrects the failed transitions
                          of flesh & blood.
Who were we before we began
                          diagramming the intransitive predicate
or implied subject of our lives,
                outlining our time inside unqualified space . . .
before we began thinking
                about our ineluctable return to stellar bits,
to whatever is next
        to nothing?
                      Yet somehow, my heart's still in it,
sunlight blotted from the corners of the sea,
                          some little meaning
obscure in the footnotes
            of our breath
                      beside the dahlias and birds
of paradise
        and a breeze lifting over the tops of mulberry
and catalpa trees
            with heart-shaped, yellow leaves.
                            Every uncertainty
still riding out the longhand of dusk,
                    our heads bent to our desks
practicing penmanship
            50 years ago—
                      smoky locomotive loops
and flourishes,
            sentences and boiler plate like cloudbanks of eternity

smudged

        in our Palmer Method books . . .
                              like noun determiners,
a spliced scrum of particles swimming out
                        the transoms,
fading with the incomplete sentences of hope. . . .

              *

Cape honeysuckle, coral trees fading
                        in the mist like candles slowly
extinguished at the other end of the beach,
                        where it looks
for all the world as if the air ends . . .
                    each celestial, overlooked
diacritical mark
        with night building as we breathe in the blind freight
of atoms that compose us
                without the first idea who we are.

              *

Along the foothills, skyline
             with its invisible ink,
                        dark leaves
like slant rhymes, everything open to interpretation. . . .
                              We go on
looking up,
       no order we can be sure of, no matter
                            what we say. . . .
A few loose lines
           of stratus clouds, like the last Italian illuminations
of the 16th century
           spread across the washed-out blue
                          like angels' wings
in a master's lost annunciation . . .
                    an intimation about how long
faith holds out. . . .
               Still, I sit here, holding my breath a little longer
with the unscripted
           scrawl of stars
                 erased in the run-on speed of light. . . .

V

Soy el mismo hasta ahora

la vida es solo lo que hace
—Neruda

Standing at the edge
of the cliff,
of the world,
I'm gazing past the waves
and cypress trees,
past the islands
and past the invisible
air, out to where
my doubts haven't changed . . .
I'm hardly more bewildered
than when I was kept
after school rewriting
my capital Ss and Gs,
making loops like cloud tops
blotted above the channel . . .
my blue scrawl streaky
as every afternoon
I opened my arms
to the hard work
of hope.
      Somewhere,
I still have those copybooks,
yellow as September leaves,
the vaguest records
of comprehension. Yet if
I'd been offered a choice,
wouldn't I choose to live
in this world?
      And if I hadn't,
I'd probably have been here anyway,
sporting my dead step-father's
coat all through grad school,

a moth-bitten black and white
tweed blurring to grey
like everything else back there?
Either way, I'm here
with just a few twigs
of philosophy to rub together
for warmth again this evening,
for comfort against the swirl
of every brilliant bit
shifting in a scrum and spun
out among the aethers. . . .

And when I stop,
look up, and count to ten,
do I calm down, or see
anything more clearly?
Not a chance.
                      You can
travel the world but
where else is there to go
but home to the sea . . .
where I stood at 4, 6, or 68,
where I was called Cree,
Crisco, or Cristobal—where,
despite the white lines
of surf rewriting
everything each day,
I am the same so far.

At Caffé Puccini—Notes on my 60th Birthday

to Gerald Stern

Our juncos are either the Oregon or Mexican brand—
I can never tell. But like most birds, I occasionally
need to get out of town . . . and so drove up 101, donating
to oil companies and the stock portfolios for the 1%'s
grandkids as I went—
                        the price of a hijacked democracy,
of late capitalism. . . Up to San Francisco to see compadres—
all of us now light years away from where we started out
ragged and reckless in gas-stingy Volkswagens, sleeping
on someone's couch between the miserable jobs of youth.
No idea how I finally made it to the Fairmont Hotel,
even with discounts, where we compare aches and organs,
instead of books and the recent prize-swap insider trading
in New York?
              I take a bus to North Beach, to a table outside
Caffé Puccini and a $3 decaf, Pavarotti soaring from the counter
to sidewalk as I recall how transcendent he was—his beatific register
and range—any god listening would have given him more time,
a subject coming up more and more these days.
                                                I sit with coffee
in a big white cup, a meatless sandwich . . . I pass on the cannoli,
hoping to buy more time, to get up and down these hills on my own
two feet, with my own shortened choruses of breath—the cable cars
$5 a pop as they knew we were coming. . . .
                                            I was wondering
where in the world your new book was, so walked to that bookstore
off Columbus where everyone's been going since the '50s, and climbed
the stairs where they keep the poetry and other dangerous materials
to find that tiny dog you rescued on Ninth Street, the lost poets
and the lost loves, as well as Thom McCann and the fluoroscope,
the green and amazing bones of our feet, glowing like a bad mid-
century horror flick. And as I read through *Save The Last Dance*,
I go back to The Drifters, to my high school gym, someone
in blue taffeta, my blue surfer Sperry deck shoes—every simple
radiating thing, a glimmering azure half-life fading out.
I'm looking for which old love songs, which false-hearted

politicians we should never forget? Why not continue to curse
the lying sonsofbitches each and every day? It's never too late
to let out with something appropriate on all their houses, to up-date
my list for the top floor in a hotel fire.
                                           Wild fires have burned
half the state, my poor pal Gary evacuated 3 times from his house,
and when it was saved again, he joked that he'd dashed out the door
with just my books in his arms.
                              May we all survive
on air! I've put in time practicing . . . and years worrying,
which is my particular talent, along with writing notes
on free post cards from Caffé Puccini while praising Pavarotti's
Nessun Dorma, while waiting for the *recitatives* of light
to float a little faith my way no matter what I don't understand
about eternity, sitting here in the shade of a civic tree or two
despite my mother flying off into whatever ever-after this spring—
just a few trills and clicks from that roadrunner in her front yard
by way of a clue, just the hit & run rhythm of my heart worn down
with virus or wine—the verdict not in.
                                    I'd usually finish
my sandwich, but there are carbohydrates in everything,
not least of which is the concupiscent Italian pastry shop
only a dozen steps across the street with its nougat and 3 kinds
of cannoli, though I've mentioned them before—the glorious
temptations and confection of the world, the longing and
lack of remedy. I leave the crusts on my plate, hoping for
blackbirds to befriend, no mind-limbering comfort from
a modest glass of Zinfandel, just a short vacation where I try
to dig up any background material on the world we've lost.

Not a feather of wind off the Pacific to turn a page—
high-pressure system parked over California for the last
8 years—just the *accompagnato* of the blue, and the bells
of Washington Square amplifying the dust sifting down
from the high windows with the un-lasting and half illuminated
facts of our lives, the uninformed glory-be of our blood—
the still air, the listening, and the deliberation of wings.

From Here on Out

Today is just another day,
like yesterday—no more secrets
to keep from the sky. Memory,
just smoke drifting
across back yards.
                      I get up
from the kitchen table
and open the window—
hoping some inspiration
might float in and sidetrack me
from rows of solitaire,
remind me that I've used up
most of the luck I arrived with
on the planet, and it might be
wise not to squander the little
that's left.
              By evening
the trees will burn against
the horizon again,
spread like a blood stain
on the glass of the blue . . .
My trouble is that
I just wandered along
for so long . . . spending my time
mindful of clouds,
blasé as a *boulevardier*
in the Paris spring air.

Walking the breakwater
now, I'm wondering
what purpose there is
to the gulls arguing
around the bins,
what reason for the wind,

its occasional grey flurry
of wings?
        More and more
it looks like it's time to refold
the map to everlasting,
its crumbled edges, its increasing
dust, and admit I was taken in
by the implausible
heavens spelling out little
we'll understand before
our molecules collapse
and we can no longer
skip rope, think straight,
or walk along the beach
in the flourish and
steady force of our blood,
blindly headed back
to the concertina of the Milky Way . . .
beneath which it seems
I'd have done as well
going door-to-door
selling moonlight in a jar.

Afternoon or evening,
I know my place
on the porch, several
streets up from the beach,
from any significance
given the useless
restatement of the waves. . . .
On the sidewalk
magnolia leaves fall
like lost affidavits
of faith. My heart,
a worn filament,
is no more incandescent

than the street lamp
on the curb, than fireflies
swirling at dusk, who,
like most of us, are trying
to escape the dark . . .

Promise

How many doorways
                have I looked into
                                with no one
waiting to pass the time of day . . .
                            to discuss rain
that never falls on roses, sea-dull acacias,
                              sun-scraped lawns?
Dirt scurries this way
                then that in the street—
                              and in the study,
my school photo has a grey cobweb
                          in the background
and that has nothing
                to do with the soul.
                              The sky looks tired
of everything
          though any bird can read the map of the air—
but that gets me exactly where?

                          The only reply to my letters
expressing interest in the position
                    is dust rising from my cuffs,
settling each evening in the west—
                          sidewalk inspector,
street sweeper, bookkeeper of fallen leaves. . . .
                                Still,
someone needs to make sense of philosophy—
                            and if not,
herd sheep, take in a stray cat.
                Throw your hands up
in the face of the past
                and little more than
                            a fine powder rises
on the path
            leading to a bench outside that bar
                              where no one

notices the hopeless rucksack
        slung over your shoulder,
the one you set off with
      half a life ago, thinking
there might be something left
       in the grab bag of the blue.
Your reward
   is a glass of rough red wine served up next to
the seawall,
   salt air, some fog hanging offshore.
             Breathe in
the usual uncertainty
       grey as the sinking pearl of the sun . . .
realize you're lucky
      to be here for a time with the light
disappearing over the bay
       like the promise of a life
to come,
   a life just drifting off. . . .

Beneath a Cemetery Overlooking the Beach

Crows dive from the cypress
and sun-burnt eucalyptus,

strafe the walk and picnic tables . . .
I'd say they'd descended from

an angry star, though we're all
just stellar dust. . . . Orange peel,

fin of a gutted fish, bits of life
cast off by bins near where I sit

with my lunch, with my hunches
leaking air . . . and know as much as

the crows, given a life cross-examined
by wind and salt spray. I'm waiting

for more time to come to a conclusion,
waiting for more time to wait,

while the crows clatter and
proclaim their autocracies

of the sky, ridiculing those
who must get up and go

back to work, or those who
no longer have work, and sit here

with their beers and irresolute
silence, watching the birds hop

over plaques and memorial benches
calling *Who cares?* They live

next to death every day, and
are going to outlast most of us,

unless that red-tailed hawk swoops
in and calls their number, calls

them on their bravado before
a heaven indifferent to us all.

To Pablo

The cypress trees grow old, losing their shapes to wind,
    outlining a poetics
of absence on the promontory's edge. I'm sitting here
    in the lacy shade
of pepper trees, thinking of you, maestro, calling you back
    from the solar mists,
from the winds blowing through the empty rooms
    of eternity. Step out,
with the torch and happy sorrow of your odes, tell us death
    is less than this
undertow ripping through the surf, singing for nothing
    through our blood.
Give us a *grito* to chase the *politicos* over the cliff,
    a song to repair
each torn ligament of desire, the stitch in the side of hope,
    give us sea foam,
crusts of sunlight, anything to follow past the white caps,
    the useless irony
of every appeal. No one's fooled when we lose one comrade
    after another and have to
calculate the sorrow of empty sidewalks, chairs outside the café;
    the death of day lilies, roses.
So if we praise our shoes, shined gloriously for a Sunday stroll,
    or the two tomato plants
we raise each spring, if we proclaim a dishtowel the happy flag
    of our republic, even these
scraps of joy slip away through the blue leaves of evening,
    the light dying out
across the shore, inside of which the soul spins down
    and is gone . . .
like the air-sealed kiss of salt in spindrift above the sea.

Jardin du Luxembourg

el que tiene un honor ye no fallece!
                    —César Vallejo

Green, sun-bleached
garden chairs, chestnut leaves
brown as billfolds,
morning clouds mirrored
on the pond where no boats
are sailing toward a dream. . . .
Enough days begin here
that I'm invisible, familiar
as the chalk-colored statues
that tourists look past,
that the old, bundled strollers
circle by. . . .
                I go unnoticed
by the woman pinching bits
of stale baguette
for the insistent birds
late each afternoon.
Who I was waiting for,
the topics of our concern,
have long escaped me?

Often as not, black rains
catch me out with whoever's
out of work, stretched across
a bench, a copy of *Le Temps*
covering his face . . .
or with the one stumbling
around the gravel promenade
in broken shoes, old hat
and overcoat . . . the one
with a stormy eye,
reciting a childhood rhyme

beneath a grey alphabet
of clouds.
    I don't have a prayer
for the wretched fellow
with torn sleeves, wearing
the same necktie all year
without shame.
     Mercy on the man
picking through the trash,
on the falling camphor leaves,
mercy on my only pair of shoes
shined on my coat sleeve,
mercy on those whose comfort
is found here among wet twigs
and decaying monuments,
the marigolds and asters
withered with autumn.
Mercy on the old-timer
tapping his watch, holding it
to his ear, looking up,
listening for God.
Mercy on us all—so little
standing between suffering
and an empty path to the stars.

All the While

> *The bare branches pointing to the place*
> *Where there's time for everything*
> —*Amichai*

The sky's a blank sheet
but for the footnotes
of cloud at the bottom,
unreadable as ever. . . .
I lived back there
in a mid-century grey—
from our street to the beach,
from the tide-pools and fog-
ghosted shore, to the roar
and riptide of surf
where I knew no better
than to be content.   Now,
when I take an early drink,
the past rolls in like fog . . .
there are the avocado trees
where I climbed into the sky,
and a bit farther off
my mother and I riding
the train to Louisville
each summer, where her parents
were still alive . . . history,
just one thing after another—
how little time we had for it.

We were only kids
when the crows started
clacking out our epitaphs
from the pines, and in this
they resembled the nuns
at school, who recanted nothing

they'd threatened us with
the day before as they forecast
our demise to darkness and/
or fire—to dust, sulfur,
burning salt.
                    Going nowhere
for so long, I was, nonetheless,
happy to be doing so. . . .
Afternoons, I stood on the cliff
conducting the up-drafts,
soundless stanzas of wind
I never translated
to any purpose beyond
the undertow of October.
How many stars died
while I looked out the window
working out the long division
of the blue, watching the acacias
blossom and wondering about
my return to some glittering
cosmic bits?
                    For the time being,
I'm content beside jasmine
and cape honeysuckle, recalling
the scented air of Babylon rising
from the hanging gardens
in our Bible History books . . .
as, all the while, we were moving
steadily toward extinction
as coherently as the six blind men
encountering an elephant
for the first time.
                    In the next
instant, I'll take in a stream of atoms
breathed out by Democritus,
who invented them, or from
the last slave hauling a stone

up a ramp on the pyramid at Giza,
or even from Po Chu-i
who survived nine emperors,
holding his breath, hoping
to outlast exile, hoping after
his next cup of wine to be
recalled to the world. . . .

Prophets, mystics,
research scientists,
who's resolved the formula
for the infinite
                    nothing
we look out to each night?
I have as little now as ever
insofar as a vision of hope obtains.
Yet, I'm still tossing ideas
into the air, from one hand
to the other, my only recourse
a hollyhock or house finch,
the evening wreckage of clouds,
suggesting something beyond empty
branches, something that might
shift the grey cells and keep
my consciousness floating
with the dust hovering above
paths in the park.
                    And for nothing
more substantial than the sound
and easygoing grace of it,
I say *Aurora Borealis*
as I did all those years ago
in General Science, though
even the outermost edges
are invisible from here,
the swirled signatures
of electromagnetic light

that might hint at
what our one precinct
in the mostly empty dark
will come to.
                     It's hard to see
the purpose of the world,
or the need . . . there's no
breadcrumb trail across
the night, no streaks
of shooting stars leading to
anything—not the least
of which might be a murmur
from the nearest spheres,
a blank passage in the oldest scrolls . . .
no cosmic cantata as Pythagoras had it
rings true. We have only the trees
still making way for wind, the dry
leaves of eucalyptus like swarms
of dead souls let go again—little change,
one year, one sky to the next. . . .

ABOUT THE AUTHOR

Christopher Buckley's recent books—in addition to ONE SKY TO THE NEXT—are *AGNOSTIC*, Lynx House Press; *The Pre-Eternity of the World*, Stephen F. Austin State Univ. Press, & *The Consolations of Science & Philosophy*, Lynx House Press.

Among over a dozen critical collections and anthologies he has edited: *On the Poetry of Philip Levine: Stranger to Nothing*, 1991; *A Condition of the Spirit: The life & Work of Larry Levis* (with Alexander Long) 2004; *Bear Flag Republic: Prose Poems & Poetics from California,* (with Gary Young) 2008; and *Messenger to the Stars: A Luis Omar Salinas New Selected Poems & Reader*, (with Jon Veinberg), 2014. The most recent are: *The Long Embrace: Contemporary Poets on the Long Poems of Philip Levine*, Lynx House Press, 2020; and *NAMING THE LOST: THE FRESNO POETS—Interviews & Essays*, Stephen F. Austin State Univ. Press, 2021.

Buckley's work was selected for Best American Poetry 2021. He was a Guggenheim Fellow in Poetry for 2007-2008 and has been awarded a Fulbright Award in Creative Writing to the former Yugoslavia, four Pushcart Prizes, two awards from the Poetry Society of America, and NEA grants in poetry for 2001 and 1984. He received the Vern Rutsala Poetry Prize from Cloudbank books for *The Far Republics* in 2017; The Lascaux Prize for *Back Room at the Philosophers' Club* in 2015; and the Tampa Review Prize for Poetry from the Univ. of Tampa Press for *Rolling the Bones* in 2009.

Over the last 40 years his poetry has appeared in *APR, POETRY, FIELD, The Georgia Review, The Iowa Review, TriQuarterly, The Kenyon Review, The Sewanee Review, Ploughshares, The New Yorker, The Nation, Northwest Review, The North American Review, The Hudson Review, The Gettysburg Review, Plume, Prairie Schooner, The Southern Review, Five Points, New Letters, The Threepenny Review, The Harvard Review,* & *Birmingham Poetry Review.*